KV-576-372

Contents

FRANCES USHER

THE *River* *runs* TO *End* OF *time*

Illustrated by
Chris Molan

OXFORD
UNIVERSITY PRESS

OXFORD

UNIVERSITY PRESS

Great Clarendon Street, Oxford OX2 6DP

Oxford University Press is a department of the University of Oxford.
It furthers the University's objective of excellence in research, scholarship,
and education by publishing worldwide in

Oxford New York

Auckland   Cape Town   Dar es Salaam   Hong Kong   Karachi
Kuala Lumpur   Madrid   Melbourne   Mexico City   Nairobi
New Delhi   Shanghai   Taipei   Toronto

With offices in

Argentina   Austria   Brazil   Chile   Czech Republic   France   Greece
Guatemala   Hungary   Italy   Japan   Poland   Portugal   Singapore
South Korea   Switzerland   Thailand   Turkey   Ukraine   Vietnam

Oxford is a registered trade mark of Oxford University Press
in the UK and in certain other countries

British Library Cataloguing in Publication Data
Data available

ISBN-13: 978 0 19 915958 1
ISBN-10: 0 19 915958 0

3 5 7 9 10 8 6 4 2

Printed in the UK by Ashford Colour Press Ltd

Available in packs
Year 5/ Primary 6 Pack of Six (one of each book)   ISBN 0 19 915963 7
Year 5 / Primary 6 Class Pack (six of each book)   ISBN 0 19 915964 5

Historical Note

This story is set in early 1645. Civil war has been raging across England for over two years. On one side, King Charles I and his Royalists; on the other, those who believed in a strong parliament that could control the King.

Civil wars tear a country apart and often divide families and friends. Ordinary people can only try to survive harsh wartime conditions and roaming armies.

It is against this background that the story of Carey and Hester Bourne and Maria and Nat Harley takes place.

Chapter One

Carey Bourne brought the ferry close to the river bank and lifted his oars for a moment, watching the drips fall. Then he stowed the oars away, flicked the mooring rope round its post and stepped out onto the landing stage, carrying the bucket of pig meal.

He picked his way across the rough grass, swinging the bucket and whistling. It was midday, but still scarcely light. Carey was used to dark winter days and didn't notice them, any more than he noticed the wet seeping through the holes in his shoes.

He glanced up at the grey January sky.

A sharp little east wind stirred against his face.

"A cold time's coming," he thought. "Snow, maybe."

He thought about it as he walked on towards the pigsty. How would he and his sister Hester manage if blizzards came? There'd be no ferry passengers. Folk wouldn't venture out, especially the old people who were the ones mainly left since the war began.

He and Hester depended on the money Carey earned from the ferry, now Father was away fighting. And Mother's accident...

Last autumn, she'd been picking apples and had fallen from the orchard ladder and hit her head. Now she sat all day in the chimney corner, not speaking, her mind muddled. Carey and Hester had sent a message to Father with a passing fairman, but Father hadn't come. Perhaps he never would.

How would Carey manage if it snowed?

It wasn't just the ferry. Their vegetables would freeze in the ground and their animals might die.

Then he remembered Miller Harley and his missis, and young Nat and Maria, across the river at the mill. The Harleys were good friends, always ready with a helping hand. Miller Harley had given him this pig meal.

"Here, pig." Carey stooped to look in the sty. "See what I got you..."

He stopped. It was too quiet. No snuffling and grunting. The sty was empty.

Where was that pesky pig?

He saw how it had escaped. Someone had wrenched off the extra plank he'd nailed on to strengthen the sty. The pig only had to push hard. Only natural.

"Pig." He looked all round. "Come, pig, come."

Not a sound, not a sign. Cursing under his breath, Carey set out to search for it.

* * *

He looked everywhere, calling all the time. Down by the river, up near the cottage, round the little orchard.

No pig.

Then he looked at the high hedge marking the boundary between their own land and the Manor next door. A determined pig could easily squeeze through.

He stood on tiptoe by the hedge, parted

the branches and called again.

"Pig. Here, pig..."

Someone on the other side laughed, someone down there, sitting in the Manor ditch. Two men.

Carey peered through the hedge. One man wore a large purple plumed hat. The other stared up at him with amused brown eyes under a tangle of long red hair.

"Upon my soul, Adam," drawled a

voice from under the hat. "We are spied upon."

"We sit peacefully, and a spying whelp appears..."

"And dares call us pig."

"Should he not be ear-cropped, Denzil?"

"Or dipped in the river there..."

"I called you nothing," protested Carey. "I called to my lost pig."

As he spoke, he saw the pig, a hundred yards away under a giant oak, its head down, rooting at something.

The two men followed his eyes.

"Ha, we shall assist you, young sir." The purple-hatted one stood up and dusted his clothes. "A chase. I love a chase."

Carey hesitated.

"You are on Sir John's land," he said. "He does not tolerate poachers."

"Poachers?" exclaimed the red-haired man. "We are here at Sir John's invitation."

"In winter quarters for a while. Unfortunately, His Majesty's forces are temporarily a trifle pressed for cash at present..."

"So we are forced to forage for our breakfast. Now, young man, a deal. We help recapture your fine pig. You lead us to a plump pheasant or two."

"Or even a humble rabbit."

Carey stared at them.

"You're King's officers," he said at last.

"Indeed." The purple hat was swept off. "Captains Denzil Brooking and Adam Hathaway. At your service."

So that was it. They were part of a Royalist company who'd been allowed by Sir John to use the Manor as winter quarters. Everyone knew Sir John was a King's man, the only one in the neighbourhood.

Carey had no thought of the pig now.

"I bid you good morning," he said.

"Wait." Captain Brooking leaned over

the hedge. "We shall wish to visit Salisbury now it is in the King's hands. How does one cross the river?"

A pause.

"By ferry," said Carey.

"Operated by...?"

"I am ferryman now," said Carey. "My father is away from home."

"Fighting for His Majesty?"

"For Parliament."

Captain Brooking regarded him thoughtfully.

"You will need business in these hard times, then. We shall use the ferry, and pay well – once our funds arrive. And we'll need other things…"

"No." Carey backed away. Then he spun on his heel and began to run. Behind him, he thought he heard laughter.

* * *

A damaged sty, a lost pig, seemed nothing now, thought Carey as he ran. A King's company wintering next door!

Well, this was Parliament country. Nobody would work for the King. Especially not the Bournes, who'd run the ferry here, father and son, for generations. Like all their neighbours, the Bournes believed in Parliament, in the people's power against the King.

"Hester! Where are you, girl?"

Carey pounded up the little path and threw the cottage door open.

"Hester, some thieving weasel's broke the sty and the pig's out. And now a King's company is wintering in the Manor..."

Seeing Maria and Nat, he stopped. He'd forgotten he'd rowed them across early today to help Hester with washday.

"A King's company?" Nat Harley jumped from his stool. "Where?"

"Hush, Nat," said Maria, turning from the washtub.

"Brother, close that door at once."
Hester crouched at their mother's side in

the chimney corner, trying to feed her with a spoon. "Do you want Mother to take chill?"

"Sorry."

Carey pushed the door shut. His mother's head jerked up. She thrust away the spoon.

"Oh, there," said Hester. "Look what you've done, brother. Now she'll take no more dinner, I know it. On such a cold day too."

Chapter Two

That afternoon, the wind was like a knife.

"Share my cloak." Maria draped it round Hester. "Now, where is this pig?"

"Show us quickly," said Hester. "I mustn't leave Mother long."

"In there." Carey pointed through the hedge. "But take care for the Royalists."

"Royalists!" said Hester scornfully. "Lift me up."

Carey hoisted her up.

"I see her. Under the trees." She clicked her tongue invitingly. "Back you come, Lovage, my naughty maid. Back home to your warm sty, Lovage."

Carey snorted and dropped her. "Lovage! Why do you give names to beasts and birds?"

"Best just call them 'pig' and 'hens'." Nat hopped up and down, trying to see over the hedge. "One day Lovage will be hams and bacon hanging from the cottage ceiling."

"I don't give them people's names," said Hester. "Only herb names."

"I should hope not," said Carey severely. "People have souls. I hope you do not say pigs and hens have souls."

Hester ignored him. She liked herbs. Old Margery Pinchin, who lived along the river bank, had taught her about herbs. And she liked calling "Yarrow" and "Parsley" to the hens at feeding time. They'd had four pigs once, including a good-natured boar called Borage. He and Lovage had had litters of piglets that Father took over the ferry to Salisbury market to sell.

That was in the old days. Now Borage was no more and Lovage was alone.

"Let me look." Nat climbed on Carey's shoulders. "Oh, the soldiers are putting up lines of tents."

"Shout to them," said Hester. "They'll chase Lovage this way. We must catch her."

"No." Carey swung Nat to the ground. "We'll not ask King's men for help."

Hester frowned. "Why not?"

"They're enemy. Father would say so."

"You don't know what Father would say."

"I do. We'll have nothing to do with them."

"Carey..."

"I'm the man of the family now, Hester, and I say we won't."

In the silence, a bell clanged from the river, metal on metal.

"The ferry." Carey started to run.

Nat ran after him. "I'll take an oar with you."

"Mind you bring that pig back," Carey shouted over his shoulder.

Hester looked at Maria.

"Take no note of Carey," she said. "Why should we do as he says?"

* * *

Carey was impossible to talk to sometimes. Hester could have told him she'd removed that plank from Lovage's sty this morning, but why should she? There was no firewood and she and Maria had been trying to wash clothes in cold water. Mother was shivering. Carey didn't understand how hard it was to look after Mother. He should have felt her chilled hands today.

"Never mind, the plank made a lovely blaze," Maria comforted her.

"I know. But what a fuss Carey made. Without the fire we'd die."

The two girls stood leaning against the boathouse, watching the ferry return from taking a woman across the river. Carey and Nat pulled an oar each, and Carey's voice came clearly over the water:

The river runs so fast today,
Pull, my friend, and pull.
We'll come through storm and
tempest when
The river's running full.

And now Nat was joining in with his high treble:

The river runs so deep today,
Wait, my friend, and wait.
We'll come to you at last, my friend,
However long and late.
The river runs to end of time,
Row, my friend, and row...

"You won't die," said Maria. "Remember we're there across the river in the mill. You only have to call us. Like this."

She took the hammer tied to the willow by the landing stage, and struck the heavy piece of iron hanging alongside. A hollow clang rang across the water. Maria laughed.

"See Carey and Nat quicken their oars? They think we are passengers summoning them."

"I wish we were," said Hester. "That would put a penny in our purse. It's been hard since Father left."

"Have no fear," said Maria. "Mother and Father would never let you starve. They promised your father when he went away. The Bournes and Harleys will always be friends. Always."

* * *

They hunted for wood along the river bank, and piled it up in the cottage garden.

"'Tis little enough," said Carey, "and wet too."

"I saw a tree in the Manor grounds, black from a lightning strike." Hester was on her knees, digging a turnip from the cold ground. "That would give good kindling. If we ask the soldiers…"

"I'll go." Nat jumped up.

"No." Carey caught his jerkin.

"But I want to see the soldiers closer. Royalists like them called at the mill yesterday. They told Father they'd captured Salisbury. They asked for–"

"Help me with this saw," Carey said shortly.

Abashed, Nat took the other end of the big double-handed saw, and they all worked quietly for a while. The girls chopped turnips for Hester to boil for supper to eat with the cheese Miller Harley had sent over that morning.

It was nearly dusk when Maria glanced up.

"Look who comes."

An odd little procession was picking its way across the field. Two tall men led the way, while a shorter one in a dented helmet was dragging along a pig by a scarlet sash.

"Lovage!" Hester ran to meet them.

"Hand the lady her property, Corporal Poyntz." The tallest man pulled down his

purple hat. "Faith, what weather!"

"I thank you, sir," said Hester, taking the sash from the grinning Poyntz. "I'll just put Lovage in her sty, and bring back the sash."

"Tomorrow morning will do." The red-haired one was examining his muddy boots ruefully. "When we come to the ferry."

"Our pay has arrived. Six of us will go to Salisbury tomorrow, on the first ferry across."

"And purchase some cheese and butter from you too."

Hester's heart thumped. Six men across in the morning: threepence. Six back at night: another threepence. She'd sell them Miller Harley's cheese, and take butter from her sparse winter store. How much would they pay?

Carey stepped forward. He was very pale.

"Captain Brooking, Captain Hathaway. We thank you for returning our pig. But the ferry will not be available to you, tomorrow or any other day. There is a bridge six miles upstream."

Nat pulled at his sleeve. "It's been blown up, Carey. To stop the pursuit. The Royalists told Father when he sold them bread yesterday."

Carey turned away.

"Then you must stay this side," he said to Captain Brooking. "Come, Nat, Maria. Your father will expect you home before dark."

"But I want to ask them..."

"I said, 'Come!'"

Hester went on standing there, holding Lovage on the red sash.

"So." Captain Brooking let out his breath in a cloud of vapour. "That is how the land lies."

"Yes." Hester raised her eyes to him, and to Captain Hathaway and Corporal Poyntz behind. "But perhaps it will change."

"Oh yes, it will change," said Captain Brooking. "We shall see to that."

Chapter Three

Carey was dreaming.

Soldiers were hurrying him through a dark forest. If only they would stop shouting...

He opened his eyes. The daylight was strange, eerie. And someone *was* shouting, and hammering.

He wrapped his blanket about him and stumbled to the door.

"I slept late," he mumbled. "I'll come to the ferry shortly."

He stopped, seeing Captain Hathaway and, behind him, whirling white snowflakes.

"For mercy's sake let me in." Captain Hathaway strode to the hearth and stirred the embers with his boot, shaking snow from his shoulders. "I have been sent to talk to you."

"I told you," Carey said quickly. "I'll have no Royalist soldiers in my ferry."

"Think sense, man. You need money. You..."

He turned. Hester was standing in the doorway, a heavy bucket in each hand. Captain Hathaway went and took them from her.

"An icy day for visiting the well," he said. "Where shall I

take these, mistress?"

"No." Hester barred his way to the next room. "I mean, thank you. But I have to wash my mother. I'll manage."

The Captain looked at Carey again.

"A sister and sick mother to care for? Don't try to stand out against His Majesty's forces. We could take your boat over at any time. Why not work with us and ease life for your family? Everyone else will."

"Nobody will. We support Parliament. My father fights for them."

"I think your father would wish you to obey your elders. Besides, he may have changed sides by now. Plenty do."

"Not Father. Now go."

Captain Hathaway went to the door. Then he turned back.

"So, nobody will work with us? What of your friends we saw yesterday? They live across the river at the mill, I believe."

"What of them?"

"Nothing," said the captain. "But I hear the miller is a sensible man. I'm sure he has trained his children in obedience. Now, for the last time. Will you put your ferry at our disposal?"

"I will not."

"Then you must bear the consequences. Good day."

*　*　*

It snowed all morning. Carey sat hunched in the boathouse, watching the flakes falling softly into the dark water. Two swans paddled mournfully past into the mist.

The bell on the further shore clanged.

"Coming," he shouted, casting off the rope. The snow half blinded him as he rowed, clinging to his eyelashes.

"Well, young man." It was Miller Harley. He grasped the prow of the boat. "Here's a day to freeze your innards. Where would we be without our ferry?

Drop the sacks down to me, Nathaniel. Carefully."

"Yes, Father." Nat grinned at Carey, and lowered four heavy sacks to his father.

"Now back to the mill and your shovelling, Nathaniel. I want that meal bin clear this afternoon."

He looked at Carey.

"Ply your oars, young man. I have business on the other side that cannot wait."

Carey rowed in silence, his eyes on the sacks at the miller's feet. Miller Harley sat brushing at the snowflakes like flies in summer.

The moment the boat bumped against the landing stage he jumped up, setting the boat rocking.

"Take these, my man."

Carey looked up. Corporal Poyntz was on the landing stage.

"Got it, sir." He took a sack from the miller. "And the next one."

"Don't drop them."

"Never fear." He took the third sack. "These'll be with Cap'n Brooking and his friends within the hour."

"Good."

"And this, sir..." He handed over a paper. Miller Harley read it, smiling.

"Of course I can," he said. "Tell them I'll send them across tomorrow."

"Very good, sir." Poyntz sketched a salute. The miller sat expectantly.

"Oh, I near forgot." The corporal reached into his doublet. "With Cap'n Brooking's compliments." He vanished with the sacks.

Miller Harley unwrapped the small package of money and began counting it. Then he caught Carey's eye and stuffed it into his sleeve.

"Ready," he said.

Carey didn't move.

"I said, 'Ready', young man. I must get back to the mill to see to affairs there."

Slowly, Carey began rowing.

"Those sacks," he said.

Miller Harley shrugged. "A few comforts for fighting men in this plaguey weather. Some French wine. Tobacco. This army pays well. What of it?"

"You didn't ask me if I would have it on

board."

Miller Harley's head went up.

"I'll carry what I like when I go from home, young man. What mean you, that I should ask?"

"They're enemy," said Carey. "King's men."

"King's men, Parliament men; what's the difference?" said the miller. "Life is costly. I have children to rear."

"My father too," said Carey. "But he thinks helping to win this war more important. Why didn't you enlist with him? You used to complain about the King often enough."

"You insolent cub." The miller tightened his fists. "By thunder, you grow above yourself since John Bourne went away. Let me tell you, it matters not who wins a war. What matters is earning a living and looking after your family. Think on that, or you'll have no living to earn and your family will starve."

They'd reached the landing stage. Miller Harley scrambled out.

"Here." Carey lifted the sack that remained under the miller's seat. "You forgot to hand this over."

The miller looked down at him.

"That one's for you," he said. "Another cheese and some smoked fish I thought you three could have for supper."

Carey's mouth watered, but he swung the sack out and dropped it at the miller's feet.

"Oh don't be so stiff-necked, lad. Take it."

"I can't," said Carey. "We are on opposite sides now." He dipped his oar and turned the boat away.

Chapter Four

It didn't stop snowing till the next afternoon.

Hester was restless. She kept thinking of what Captain Hathaway had said about Maria and Nat, that they would do whatever their father told them.

But did it matter if they helped the Royalists? Carey was so stubborn. Working for the soldiers would help them so much.

"I'm going out," she said.

"Where?" Carey stood looking out of the cottage window.

"Just a walk. Downstream a little way."
She bent to kiss Mother. Mother's blue
eyes looked up anxiously into Hester's,
and she said something.

"I'll not be long. Carey will look after
you."

She and Mother used to go for walks
along the bank together, talking all the
way. That's what Hester missed most.
Talking to Mother.

She pushed the door open against the
heavy drift of snow outside, and turned to
look up at the cottage roof, weighted
down with a thick white covering. Then
she ran down the field, feet slithering,
sending up flurries of snow. As she reached
the river, the sun broke through. Instantly,
the world was shimmering and sparkling
like diamonds.

"Oh!" Hester drew deep breaths of the
cold clean air.

At that moment, an idea came to her.

Glancing guiltily back at the cottage,

she began walking along the bank, facing upstream, hurrying towards the Manor.

A group of soldiers lounged at the Manor gates. One barred her with a pike.

"You got business in this camp, miss?"

She cleared her throat. "Yes."

"With?"

Who should she say? Not an officer.

"Um... Corporal Poyntz."

The man stepped back and turned his head.

"Hey, Poyntz. Lady to see you."

"Afternoon, miss." Corporal Poyntz pushed forward. He tipped back his dented helmet and looked down at her quizzically. "Here's a surprise. Looking for my friend Lovage again, are you?"

*　*　*

On the way home, Hester was almost skipping, her heart was so light. It'd done her good, an hour sitting on an upturned box with Corporal Poyntz and his friends, helping to polish their equipment, listening to their stories, laughing at their jokes. There hadn't been many jokes at home lately.

She stopped on the river path and laid down her bundle of blackened wood. She felt under her cloak. Yes, the packages were all still there: a plum pie, half a haunch of venison, a piece of gingerbread and – most wondrous of all – a tiny flask of brandy.

"Not for you, mind," Poyntz had warned. "Just a sip now and then for your Ma. From what you told me, she needs it."

He'd brushed away her thanks.

"Just sharing out what comes my way." He gave her an enormous wink. "Why should officers get it all? It's look out for yourself in wartime, that's what I say. Now, you hop out under here."

He'd looked over his shoulder, then held up the fence wire for her.

"Not much harm in firewood. But keep the rest of that stuff under your cloak, miss, else you know what'll happen to me." He'd run a grubby finger across his throat and laughed again.

Of course there was no harm in it. Once Carey saw how generous the soldiers could be if you were friendly to them instead of hostile, he'd see sense. Wouldn't he?

She'd smiled up at Poyntz.

"Perhaps I'll see you and the officers using the ferry tomorrow," she had said.

To her surprise, Poyntz hadn't smiled back.

"The ferry. I don't think so, miss. Sorry. You just enjoy that stuff while you can."

She was nearly home before she found out what he'd meant. The sun was setting red behind the willows when a barge glided past her, towed by two large horses plodding along the opposite bank.

Barges often plied their way along here, laden with stone from the quarries. But this barge was empty. And somehow the horses were different: glossier, more military looking. And weren't those Royalist soldiers astride, and others walking alongside?

Hester hurried on, oddly uneasy. As she rounded the last bend, she saw Carey on

the landing stage.

"Hester, quickly."

"What's happening?" She started to run.

"Can't you see?"

He pointed. Across at the mill, they were tying the barge to another already moored there. Even as she watched, a third

barge rounded the bend and loomed up through the twilight.

"What is it?"

"They're building a bridge of boats. They've commandeered those barges and they're building a bridge of boats." Carey's voice was hard. "So they won't need the ferry. Nobody will."

"But that'll ruin us," whispered Hester. "We won't have any money."

"I know. And look at the first barge."

Hester strained her eyes in the dusk.

"Nat? Talking to the soldiers?"

"Helping them, more like. He's been holding stuff for them, carrying their tools. And Maria..."

Hester felt sick.

"What about Maria?"

"Maria and her mother brought out drinks for them. All laughing together."

"But... they're our friends. They wouldn't help the army take our living away."

The Harleys wouldn't betray them like that.

"See for yourself."

Laughter floated across the water.

Suddenly, Hester was angry, angrier than she'd been in her whole life.

"Traitors! They're traitors, working against us like that." She stamped her foot and the packages spilled out and rolled into the river. "How can they?"

Maria knew they needed money to feed Mother and keep her warm. All the Harleys knew that.

She turned from the river and walked away, swallowing down her angry tears.

"It's war now," she shouted over her shoulder. "War. Bournes against Harleys. And the Bournes are going to win. You'll see."

Chapter Five

For a week the weather froze hard and the millpond bore a sheet of ice.

Then one night the wind swung to the south. By morning, thawing snow dripped from the mill roof. At the top of the building Maria sat on the floor, her arm round the mill cat, looking out of the low window.

She loved the mill. The sound of water splashing and squirting through the wooden blades of the wheel, the thud of machinery rocking the building, had been the background to her whole life. But this winter was different. The soldiers had come.

She could see them down there now in the rain. The barges were lashed tightly together, and soldiers passed backwards and forwards along the plank walkways. Villagers too.

Today the army was erecting a wooden handrail. She could see Nat down there, helping, wearing Corporal Poyntz's dented helmet.

"Maria!"

Maria jumped up. The cat fled. She leaned over the wooden rail and saw her mother three floors below, looking up.

"Here, Mother."

"Help me take this ale to the soldiers."

"Yes, Mother."

What could she do but obey?

Heads bent against the rain, they carried out the tankards.

"Mind the soldiers pay," warned her mother. "None of their remittance notes.

They'll try it with you, but you must tell them."

"Yes, Mother."

Maria moved along the soldiers, handing out ale and taking money.

"Ah, Mistress Maria."

Captain Brooking was by the landing stage, not wearing his purple hat today, but very correct and military in full uniform.

"Tell me, has your father procured the cask of wine I requested? And my new boots?"

"He has them ready."

"And the gloves?"

"Yes, sir. The glover stitched all night."

The captain smiled.

"Folk in these parts have good business sense."

"Not all folk," said Maria.

He followed her eyes across the river. The ferryboat lay at its moorings, empty and idle, with Carey and Hester beside it, talking.

Captain Brooking shrugged.

"Foolish. They could have made themselves a little richer. But..." He gestured at the bridge of boats, thronged with people, "... nobody needs them now."

Maria's heart twisted.

"I'll go and talk to them," she said. She leaned past him and struck the ferry bell.

A roar of laughter went up.

"She wants the ferryboat!"

"The ferryboat!"

"We got the army bridge now."

"And nothing to pay!"

Captain Brooking said softly, "I think they will not come for you, those two. They turned their backs when they saw who summoned them."

"I know."

She left him and went and found Nat.

"Take this money back to the mill, and go and shovel grain for Father. I'm going across the river."

He stared up at her.

"How?"

"On the bridge of boats. There's no other way."

* * *

Nat shovelled a little grain, and slipped out again to swing on the newly-made handrail. "I hope the war goes on for years," he said. "I can't wait to join the army."

"You can get off there first," said Poyntz, "before you break it. And I'll have my helmet back. It's raining."

He sat on a barge roof and lit his pipe. Nat climbed up beside him.

"Know how my helmet got dented like this?" asked Poyntz after a time.

"No."

"Terrible battle up near Bath in '43." Poyntz drew on his pipe. "We was marching uphill straight towards the muskets. They mowed us down in hundreds. Had to flee in the end. Then, when we thought we was safe, an ammunition wagon blowed up. Right in our midst."

"Go on." Nat was wide-eyed.

"That's it. I was the lucky one. That's all I done." He tapped his helmet. "My mate lost his arm. Three got blinded. Two weren't never found."

In the silence, Poyntz levered himself to his feet.

"Don't talk about what you don't understand, young Nat," he said. "Yes, you can laugh with your mates. But, deep down, war's terrible. And civil war – brother fighting brother and friend fighting friend – that's the worst. Take it from me. I know."

* * *

Maria wished she hadn't come. She sheltered in the boathouse with Carey and

Hester, and couldn't think of anything to say.

"Do you have passengers? I mean – some people must…"

"Oh, some," said Hester. "Carey goes often to the village to ask people to use the ferry instead of the bridge."

"Plenty of people promised at first they would," said Carey.

"And?"

"Some still do."

"If Carey's in the village, I row them now," said Hester.

They watched Butcher Haycraft shepherd his family past the boathouse. When they saw them watching they hurried on towards the bridge.

"Margery Pinchin uses the ferry," said Hester. "And Thomas at the forge."

"'Course, Thomas is a Parliament man. One of us." Carey looked at Maria. "Like Miller Harley was once."

Silence.

"I can't stop my parents trading with the enemy," Maria said, head down.

"You can try," said Hester fiercely.

Another silence. Then Maria got up and left.

She was nearly at the bridge when she heard someone running.

"I'll row you over," said Carey.

"I've no money."

"No matter. Get in."

She watched him bending to the oars.

The rain beat on the water.

"We'll have floods soon," he said.

"Yes." Three years ago, the river had risen and poured through the mill. The Bournes had rowed over somehow and helped haul meal sacks to the top floor.

At the landing stage Carey held the boat steady, not looking at Maria.

"Carey," she said. "How's your mother?"

Carey looked up.

"Better. She sits straighter and copies what we say, lately."

"I'm glad."

She climbed out of the boat.

"Carey..."

"I'm not changing," he said.

"I know. But one day the war will end."

He nodded.

"And we'll all be friends again," she called, but he'd pulled the boat round and was already rowing away.

Chapter Six

During February it seemed the rain would never stop. It washed the snow away and the river rose and burst its banks. Bubble-strewn water swept past the mill and the boathouse, tumbling branches and debris on a headlong rush to the sea.

"It will go down soon," Hester said to Mother, combing her hair one afternoon. She often talked to Mother even now. "And we are safe and snug indoors."

"Snug." Mother smiled. "Snug indoors."

Over Mother's head, Hester met Carey's

worried eyes. Yesterday they'd dragged the ferryboat up to the cottage door to keep it from washing away. Today the water was still rising.

What if the cottage flooded? When it had happened before, Mother and Father had hurried everyone up to the loft with all their possessions, to wait till the water receded. Now Hester eyed the loft ladder uneasily. Could she and Carey lift Mother between them?

She turned her thoughts away. What could they have for supper? She pictured Corporal Poyntz's venison longingly, swirling somewhere at the bottom of the river. No matter. They were better off without army gifts. They still had bread and a little cheese. And now the ground was softer, Carey could dig out turnips again.

"Good hot turnip stew for supper today, Mother," she said cheerfully.

Mother made a face.

"Mutton broth is better," she said.
Carey's head turned sharply.
"What?"

Hester swallowed. "She said, mutton broth is better. And it is, Carey, much better. Remember Mother's mutton broth in the old days?"

Carey was still staring at his mother.

"She wasn't copying. She was speaking her own words, Hester. She's never done that since she fell."

"I know." Hester knelt at Mother's side and looked deep into her eyes. "Mother? Please. Say more."

She watched Mother working, making words come.

"Hester," she said at last, very carefully. "Good girl, Hester. And Carey, good."

She reached her hand to them both, and her eyes were alive and loving.

"And mutton broth, good. Mutton broth for supper." She laughed. "Yes. Good."

So that settled supper.

"If Mother wants mutton broth," said Carey, "she must have it."

"Off to the village, Carey, and buy bones from Butcher Haycraft. Then I'll put the broth to simmer. No harm will come to us here, will it, Mother?"

Mother shook her head and smiled. Hester gave Carey the last coins from her purse.

"Don't worry. You'll make some more from the ferry soon."

"Not while the river's aflood. Madness to venture out there now."

"I know."

He hesitated in the doorway.

"Watch the river closely, Hester. It could still reach the cottage."

"Carey, will you go?"

As if in support, Lovage grunted from her makeshift pen in the corner. Fearing floods, they'd brought her in last night.

"Pesky pig." Carey pulled his hat down. "I wish Mother had demanded bacon broth for supper."

Hester looked at him, her arm round Lovage's fat neck.

"You don't," she said. "Now run. And come back quickly."

* * *

It was peaceful sitting in the cottage with Mother, sewing. The fire crackled, the rain drummed on the roof and Lovage snuffled in her straw.

"When Carey comes back, Mother, we'll make the broth quickly, and put it to cook over the fire," said Hester, laying down her needle. At that moment, a knock came at the door.

"Is Carey back so soon?"

But it was old Margery Pinchin outside, huddled under a soaking wet sack. She looked up at Hester with bright eyes.

"Where's your brother? I must cross the river straightly."

"He's gone to the village."

The old woman gripped her hand.

"'Tis mightily urgent, my dear. They come over just now on that bridge with a message for me. A mother's in trouble with a babby across there. I must go. I got all me herbs and things in this bag. Look."

"You must use the bridge, Mother Pinchin."

"I dursn't, I dursn't. The soldiers say they're taking it down directly. No, 'tis the ferry I used all me life, my dear, and I'll use it now. You must take me, Hester. 'Tis death and life."

Margery Pinchin went to the upside-down ferryboat and tried to lift its bows off the ground.

"We can turn him over between us, Hester, and drag him down to the river. I seen you out rowing lately, rowing strong. You'll get me there, my dear."

Hester looked at the old woman. Behind her, the river stretched wide, swirling madly. Only the willows, up to their necks in water, marked its true path.

"Ferrying's in your blood," said Margery Pinchin. "Come, you'll help me save this poor soul's life and her babby."

It might take longer than usual, perhaps, but still only a few minutes. She could leave Mother alone a few minutes. That's all it would take.

Chapter Seven

People were strange, Carey thought, hurrying back from the village, soaked through. Butcher Haycraft, for instance.

When Carey told him Mistress Bourne had recovered her speech so much as to ask for mutton broth, he'd insisted on finding all the good mutton bones he could, and waved any payment away.

"Just being neighbourly," he'd declared, wrapping the bones. Carey nearly asked if he could be neighbourly enough to use the ferry as he'd promised, but he didn't. There were people you could never change.

It would be good to sit by the fire and watch Mother enjoy the broth. Perhaps things really were improving at last. The soldiers would surely leave soon. Then people would use the ferry. And spring was coming...

He reached the cottage and turned to look at the river. No worse, he thought, relieved. Then his hand froze on the door.

Towards the far bank, a boat was sweeping helplessly down river. Someone aboard was thrusting at the swirling water with an oar.

"What...?"

Then he recognized it. The ferry.

"Hester?" He burst into the cottage. "Hester?"

Then he saw his mother's chair, empty, and his mother at the window, holding on tightly. She turned her head.

"Hester gone," she said. "Hester in boat."

She stared at him desperately. Then,

with a great effort, she added, "Carey, help her. Go help Hester very quickly now."

* * *

He ran down the slope without feeling the rain, without knowing his feet touched the ground. On the river bank he hesitated. Then he ran to the bridge of boats.

"Halt."

A pike was pressed in his belly. Carey looked pleadingly at the soldier.

"Let me on. Please."

"The bridge is closed. By order."

"But I must cross."

"Use the ferry."

Carey laughed mirthlessly. He seized the man's arm.

"Look there, you fool, there's the ferry."

The soldier wrenched his arm away.

"I have orders. Nobody is to cross. The bridge will be dismantled shortly."

Carey clenched his fists, then forced them to relax.

"Please," he said. "My sister is like to be swept away. Drowned. I beg you."

The sentry's face didn't change, but he moved very slightly to one side.

"Three minutes," he said. "Then it's closed."

It was enough. Carey pounded along the walkway. "Let Miller Harley be at home," he prayed. Miller Harley would help him.

He thundered over the landing stage

but, before he reached the mill, there were Maria and Nat.

"Hester's in the boat and being..." he began.

"We know. We saw her."

"She was nearly across when she lost an oar," said Nat.

"Maria, your father. Where's your father?"

"In Salisbury with Mother. Finding silks for the officers."

Carey groaned. He looked at the river. To his relief he saw the ferry a hundred yards away, caught in reeds.

"You two cross the bridge. The soldier will let you if you're quick. Run to the cottage and look after Mother. Hurry. I'll try to reach the boat on my own."

"I'll come." Maria pushed Nat towards the bridge. "It needs two to do it. And I have this rope, look."

Already Nat was halfway across the bridge.

"Quickly, Carey!"

They ran along the bank. Carey stopped and cupped his mouth.

"Hester! Can you hear me?"

He saw her look round. The boat bobbed.

"Carey! Yes."

"Who's that with her?" he asked Maria.

"Margery Pinchin."

He shook his head. He cupped his mouth again.

"Hester! Catch this line."

"Yes."

He coiled Maria's rope, ready to throw.

The boat bobbed again. Perhaps Hester and Margery Pinchin had changed places. It rocked violently, spun half round, and was free of the reeds. Then it was swept by the racing currents down river once more, heading for the big bend.

"Follow it," shouted Carey.

"No, this way." Maria was already cutting across the field. "We'll reach the

other side of the bend before the boat comes. And it's higher ground. We'll be able to see."

They ran across the field, panting.

"It comes, see?" Maria pointed.

But it was on the far side that the boat was rounding the bend.

"The rope's too short." Maria doubled up, fighting for breath, as the ferry swept past. "We can never catch it now."

Chapter Eight

The Royalists were leaving. Ordered out of their comfortable winter quarters, back to the war.

Corporal Poyntz had managed to secure a small cart by himself at the rear of the baggage train. Reins held loosely, lulled by glimpses of the flooded river, the steady clip-clop of hooves and the marching tread of less fortunate men ahead, he was content for the moment.

As usual, nobody had told him where they were going. He just hoped there wasn't a battle at the end of it.

His eyes snapped open. Something was happening across the river there.

"Whoa, whoa."

He dropped the reins and jumped down. The horse's head drooped.

Before he reached the river, he could see how things stood. A boat was sweeping out of control, with two females aboard, crying out. On the far bank, two youngsters were shouting as they tried to keep up with it.

"Hold on there."

He ran and rummaged in his cart for a good length of baggage rope. Running back, he stripped off his doublet, looping the rope around him. He drew level with the boat, then with a spurt, ahead of it. He stood panting, waiting for it, measuring the distance with his eye.

"February," he thought, "*February*," and, with a deep breath, plunged into the icy river.

It snatched his breath away. He struck

out for the boat and gripped it as it passed.
The two females hauled him, dripping and
swearing, aboard.

He shook himself like a dog and looked
at Hester.

"You," he said, through chattering
teeth. "And your brother over there."

Hester nodded.

"Can he catch a rope?"

"Of course."

Poyntz uncoiled it from his middle, and

hailed Carey on the bank. "You'd better be right."

Carey caught the flying rope first time. Then, together, all their strength pitted against the tugging current, he and Maria hauled the boat to safety.

* * *

As soon as she was ashore, Margery Pinchin hastily applied ointment to Maria and Carey's hands, sorely burnt by the rope, and bandaged them. Then she set off to her sick woman.

"I'm sorry about the ferry," said Hester.

"You'll do it next time, my dear. I told you, it's in your blood." She bustled away over the fields.

The four of them towed the ferry back to the mill against the current, as dusk fell.

"Oh, the bridge of boats," cried Hester. "It's gone."

Only two barges remained, one on each side, the river rushing between.

"We can't cross. We've only one oar."

"Easy." Poyntz disappeared into the deserted barge. "Wait there."

They listened to him wrenching wood.

"The army won't miss these little bits." He handed out rough planks. "Make very nice oars, these will."

They paddled towards the ferry landing stage as darkness fell. Carey began to sing:

> *The river runs so deep tonight,*
> *Wait, my friends, and wait...*

They joined in, even Poyntz's rumbling bass:

> *We'll come to you at last, my friends,*
> *However long and late.*
> *The river runs to end of time,*
> *Row, my friends, and row,*
> *When pain and war are long behind*
> *The river still will flow.*
> *The river runs so high tonight,*
> *Stand, my friends, and stand...*

The boat bumped against the landing stage. Poyntz scrambled out. Hester looked up and saw a light above them.

"Upon my soul, Adam," came the familiar drawl. Captain Brooking held his lantern higher and Hester saw the purple hat, and two dark figures in the shadows behind him. "The ferry runs late tonight."

Hester looked for Poyntz, remembering his horse and baggage cart abandoned somewhere on a track, and the damaged barge across the water. But Corporal Poyntz was no longer there.

"Perhaps, Denzil, they still pursue their pig." Captain Hathaway came forward. "Mayhap Mistress Lovage took to the water this time."

"'Tis very likely. But, come. You must alight."

Gallantly, Captain Brooking assisted Maria and Hester onto the landing stage, and Carey followed.

"We and our barges will be gone within

the hour." His tone had changed. "We have military business to attend to."

He turned to Carey.

"And business will return for you, young man."

"If my passengers return."

"I've observed," said Captain Brooking, "that most folk fit themselves to changing fortunes. Especially in civil war. Few are as stiff-necked as you. I was enquiring a minute ago if perhaps this runs in the family."

"Enquiring?" Carey frowned.

"Your father's been telling me..."

"My *father*?"

The third man came out of the shadows. Exhausted and travel-weary, but unmistakably the same Father who'd been away nearly a year.

"The captains and I talked while I waited for you to come home." He put his arms round Carey and Hester. "Stiff-neckedness is to be prized if it means trying

to do the right thing. We agreed, even if we fight on opposite sides. But enough of war."

They began walking up to the cottage.

"Your message took a long time to find me. But I am here – for a while, at least."

He smiled at Maria.

"When I arrived this evening, young Nat was chattering like a monkey to my wife. And sometimes receiving an answer. So – home and supper. She tells me we're to have mutton broth tonight."

About the author

I've had stories in my head all my life, but for a long time I didn't write them down. I suppose I thought I was too busy. Finally, though, I settled down as a writer and, so far, the stories keep on coming.

I first thought of *The River Runs to End of Time* perhaps because I live near an old mill. Looking at it one day, I began to see the Bournes and the Harleys, separated by a river, yet united by it, and all of them trying, whatever the war's doing to them, to stay friends.